Lawrence E. Mick

To Live as We Worship

The Liturgical Press
Collegeville, Minnesota

Cover design by ANN BLATTNER. *Illustration anonymous.*

THE LITURGICAL PRESS
Collegeville, Minnesota 56321

Nihil obstat: Robert C. Harren, *Censor deputatus.*
Imprimatur: ✛George H. Speltz, D.D., Bishop of St. Cloud.
          October 24, 1983

Library of Congress Cataloging in Publication Data

Mick, Lawrence E., 1946–
    To live as we worship.

    1. Catholic Church—Liturgy.   2. Spiritual life—
Catholic authors.   I. Title.
BX1970.M52   1983   264'.02   83-24868
ISBN 0-8146-1327-6 (pbk.)

To Live as We Worship

Contents

Preface   7

A Sacrifice of Praise   10

Always One Step Ahead   17

And Now, a Word from Our Sponsor   25

Getting It All Together   32

An Attitude of Gratitude   42

For Those Who Know How to See   49

Where Heaven and Earth Meet   59

A Pattern for Spontaneity   66

The Times of Our Lives   73

A Living Sacrifice   81

Sharing the Shared Life of God   88

The Liturgy of Life   94

Preface

A PREFACE HAS BEEN DESCRIBED as that part of a book which is written last and placed first in the book, pretending to be the author's beginning but actually being a review of what the author has managed to write, regardless of what he or she set out to write. This preface, however, is precisely what its name suggests—a word written before the book itself. In it, I wish to set out my intentions and goals, to define the project that this book represents. Whether it turns out to be an adequate forecast of what follows, the reader will have to judge.

The writing of a book is a strange and mystery-laden experience. The author struggles for months or even years to bring forth to the world this child of his or her mind and heart. The labor pains are sometimes intense and prolonged. Like any mother, the author has known this child in an intimate way for a long time, yet when the labor is over and the offspring sees the light of day, both mother and author are sometimes surprised at how the child appears.

Nevertheless, I choose to begin by describing what I hope this book will be. My goal in the following pages is to share some insights into life and liturgy that I have found stimulating and rewarding in my own spiritual growth. My fundamental conviction is that the liturgy of the Church is a rich source of both insight and inspiration for daily living. For too long we have suffered from a divorce between liturgy and life, as if the God we worship is not Lord of the rest of our lives as well.

The contemporary liturgical renewal has done much to bridge that gap. It is my prayer that this little book will, in some small measure, further that process. If reading and meditating on these pages leads the reader to a deeper integration between the experience of worship and the whole of life, then the labor pains will have been worthwhile.

My approach will be fairly straightforward. I will attempt to present in summary fashion some basic insights into the nature of the liturgical experience. This material I perceive to be generally accepted by experts in the field of liturgy; it represents the fruit of the labors of countless scholars and teachers who have preceded us. Following this summary presentation of each dimension of the worship experience, I will try to draw out some implications that seem to me to flow from each element. It is here that whatever originality this book contains will be found. These insights will not be in the nature of necessary conclusions but more in the order of tentative probings. My hope is that they will stimulate the reader to deeper reflection and insight into how the experience of worship can influence and transform the rest of our lives.

I am indebted to many people, too numerous to mention here, for the seeds they have planted in my mind that have given rise to these reflections. Special thanks are in order, though, to the members of the working group on Liturgical Spirituality of the North American Academy of Liturgy. The creative ferment that was stirred up in their meeting in January 1982 provided the inspiration and impetus to undertake this project. They bear no responsibility for what I have done with their seminal ideas, but I remain indebted to them for their willingness to share the fruits of their efforts with me.

A Sacrifice of Praise

ONCE UPON A TIME there were three trees growing on a hill. Decade after decade they grew, tall and straight and majestic. One day the first tree said, "If I ever get cut down, I want to be a baby's cradle." A decade later the second tree responded, "If I ever get cut down, I want to be made into a large boat to sail the seven seas." Years later the third tree said, "I don't want to get cut down; I just want to stand here and point men and women to God."

Years passed and then the woodsmen came. They cut down the first tree and said, "Let's make it into a feedbox for cattle." The tree protested but they made it into a feedbox and sold it to an innkeeper in Bethlehem. In time the feedbox became a cradle, and the tree was heard to say, "This is even better than I expected."

They cut down the second tree and said, "Let's make it into a small fishing boat." The tree objected, but they built a fishing boat and sold it to a Galilean fisherman named Peter. It became an important pulpit for a wandering preacher one day, and the second tree said, "This is even better than I had hoped."

Then they went toward the third tree and said, "The Romans are paying well for crosses these days." The tree protested, but they cut it down and sold it to the Romans. Jesus was crucified on it, and that tree has been pointing men and women to God for over nineteen hundred years. Thus all three trees sacrificed their lives and their plans for God's glory.

In Eucharistic Prayer IV, currently in use in the Roman Catholic tradition, the presider prays:

> Lord, look upon this sacrifice which you have given
>   to your Church;
> and by your Holy Spirit, gather all who share this
>   bread and wine
> into the one body of Christ, a living sacrifice of praise.

The prayer echoes Paul's exhortation to the Romans to "offer your bodies as a living sacrifice holy and acceptable to God, your spiritual worship" (Romans 12:1).

Among the early Christians, the term "sacrifice" was used to refer primarily to the lives they led. By righteous living and deeds of love and service, they gave glory to God in their daily existence. Their whole lives were seen as spiritual offerings, sacrifices of praise. Later the term became commonly used to apply also to the Eucharist, since that liturgical celebration was an expression of the meaning of their lives. The Eucharist celebrated the sacrifice of Jesus, his offering of himself to God as a "gift of pleasing fragrance" (Ephesians 5:2), and in the Eucharist the Christians committed themselves to live as Jesus did, offering their lives for the glory of God.

As time passed, the term "sacrifice" came to be associated almost totally with the Eucharist, eclipsing the early insight that all of our lives are to be offered to the Lord. The contemporary renewal of Scripture study and the renewal of the liturgy invite us to recapture this ancient insight as a basis of our spirituality.

Liturgy and Life

In the Constitution on the Sacred Liturgy of the Second Vatican Council, the liturgy is described as "the summit toward which the activity of the Church is directed" and "the fount from which all her power flows" (no. 10). This dual nature of the liturgy has been a seminal insight that has borne much fruit in the work of many writers and in the lives of many Christians since the council. Yet it remains true that this integral relationship between the liturgy and all of the Christian's life is only partially realized in the experience of many Church members. The liturgy should be the summit where all one's daily experiences are gathered and offered to the glory of God. It should also be the source of strength and inspiration for living out the Christian commitment on a daily basis. Like the systolic/diastolic action of the human heart, the liturgy draws us in and sends us forth continually, sustaining the life of Christ in us.

The liturgy, therefore, should serve as a sound basis for the personal spirituality of the Christian. This is not to suggest that the worship of God is simply a "tool" for another purpose. To worship the Lord is an end in itself, the highest activity in which humans can engage. Yet participation in worship on a continual basis should have an effect on the worshipers, an effect that transcends the worship experience itself. Those who regularly celebrate the liturgy together ought to be formed and shaped by constant exposure to its various elements. If the liturgy is in any sense a significant experience for those who celebrate it, then the worshipers will be changed by the experience. So, too, their spirituality should be shaped and formed in such a way that it is congruent with the themes and dynamics of the liturgy itself.

A Liturgical Spirituality

The term "spirituality" is itself often a source of confusion and misunderstanding. For too many people, the spiritual life is a compartment of their experience, carefully defined and neatly tucked away so that it can neither contaminate nor be contaminated by the rest of their lives. Spiritual matters have to do with God, church, and religion; they have no significant connection with politics, economics, professional responsibilities, career opportunities, recreation, entertainment, cultural events, family interactions, or anything else that really matters in their lives.

To speak of one's spiritual life as if it were somehow distinct from the rest of life is already to misstate the situation. We really do have only one life to live. Our spiritual life is identical to our "real" life, or else it is an unreal fantasy existing only in theory. Every life is really a spiritual life; the question is what spirit animates it.

Spirituality, therefore, is a very broad category, encompassing much more than one's prayer and formal religious practices. Spirituality is a characteristic way of approaching God and life, and it affects every dimension of one's life. There can be numerous different spiritualities or styles of spirituality. To some extent, each person's spirituality will be unique, since it is the shape of a unique individual's way of dealing with God and the universe. Yet one's spirituality will also share some common dimensions with others, to the extent that common experiences of life have been shared.

Thus, those who share liturgical experiences on a regular basis might be expected to manifest some common characteristics in the way they habitually approach the Almighty and deal with God's creation. This is what I mean by a "liturgical spirituality," a spirituality that is based upon, congruent with, and shaped by, the liturgical experience. The elements of the liturgy and the dynamics of its celebration suggest certain attitudes and ways of dealing with all of life.

Liturgy's Impact

Historically, it seems that the liturgy has always had a significant effect on the styles of spirituality among the people of God. When the liturgy began to emphasize the divinity of Christ in reaction to the Arian heresy, for example, the spirituality of the people began to rely more and more upon the saints as intercessors, since Christ was seen as a distant, unapproachable Lord. So, too, the gradual exclusion of the laity from the liturgical action through the centuries led to a spirituality that drew its inspiration from popular devotions rather than from the liturgy, which seemed foreign and proper only to the clergy.

It is not unreasonable to expect, then, that the contemporary renewal of the liturgy should have its effect on the spirituality of our own time. One of the fundamental principles of the renewal is that the liturgy is the activity of the whole people of God, clergy and laity together. As the liturgy is increasingly reclaimed by people as their own, it is to be hoped that the liturgical experience will once again become a vital foundation for a deep and vibrant spirituality. Only then can it be said that the efforts to renew our worship have borne their intended fruit.

In the chapters that follow, we will look at the liturgical experience from a variety of perspectives, noting the elements and dynamics that are integral to worship traditions of the "mainline" Churches. There are other forms of worship in other groups, but there is a general convergence among the "liturgical" Churches that enables us to describe these elements as basic to the shared tradition of liturgy among these denominations. After describing each of the elements, we will probe each to see what implications we can discover there for the way we relate to God and the world in the rest of our lives. It is important to realize at the outset, however, that spirituality does not develop one element at a time. A healthy spirituality develops organically, drawing upon the totality of the experience of life and liturgy. The limits of the written word and conceptual thought force us to deal with one element at a time here; in practice we grow much more integrally.

My perspective in this book will be based on the Roman Catholic variety of the liturgical experience, since that is the one with which I am most familiar. The principles enunciated, however, are generally applicable to all those Church traditions that cherish a formal and traditional liturgy. So, too, our primary referent will be the celebration of the Eucharist. The implications are much broader, however, and extend to other liturgical forms and sacraments as well.

Reflection Questions

1. When I think of the word "sacrifice," what images come to mind? Are they positive or negative?

2. Do I see my life as a sacrifice to the Lord? Do my daily actions give God praise and glory? How have I glorified God this day?

3. How much of my life belongs to the Lord? What do I hold back, what part of my life is still outside the Lord's rule?

4. If I were asked to describe my own personal spirituality, what would I say?

5. In what ways has my experience of the liturgy shaped my prayer life? In what ways has it influenced my outlook on the world at large?

Always One Step Ahead

"LOVE, THEN, CONSISTS IN THIS: not that we have loved God, but that he has loved us. . . . We, for our part, love because he first loved us" (1 John 4:10, 19). These verses point out one of the most basic principles of liturgy and of the spiritual life: God always has the initiative. We never get the jump on God. In more formal language, this is often called the primacy of grace, for it is God's gift to us that comes first. Our action toward God is always a reaction, a response to what God has done first.

Someone has described our situation as similar to that of a man who has fallen into a deep well. Try as he might, he cannot climb out, for the well is smooth and offers no handhold or toehold. Grace is like a rope that God lowers to rescue the trapped and helpless victim. All a person has to do is hang on. But it is God who takes the initiative and God who saves us. On our own we are all as helpless as the man in the well.

It must be admitted that this fact is not always as deeply understood as it should be. We speak so blithely of becoming a Christian or joining a Church or entering religious life, as if it were really our decision, our initiative. But it is always God who moves first, God who calls, God who invites, God who challenges. "It was not you who chose me, it was I who chose you" (John 15:16).

This is not to say that our response to God's initiative is unimportant; but it is to insist that it is always in the nature of a response. The response must be an active one, an embracing of God's will, a loving the One who has loved us first. And the response may be complex and of long duration, as in the case of a response to a life vocation. There is no room here for a simplistic approach to life that abandons responsibility on the basis that God will tell me every move to make. Yet it is important that we keep the priority clear and constantly recognize that the priority both in liturgy and in spiritual life is always God's.

Liturgy as Response

This basic fact is reflected in the liturgical experience in several ways. Even a cursory reading of the prayers and texts of the liturgy will make it clear that the whole existence of the liturgy is a response to what God has done and is doing in the world. It is because God has acted powerfully and lovingly on our behalf that we gather together for liturgy at all. It is God who has called us to be the Church, to form this assembly. In Greek the very term for "church" is *ekklesia*, those "called out." The gathering of the Church is not simply a free association of likeminded individuals, but a response to God's invitation to be a "chosen people."

The primacy of grace also shows up in the structure of our worship. Almost every liturgy begins with a Liturgy of the Word. The word of God is proclaimed as a way of remembering what God has done and as an opportunity to hear that word as it applies to the present situation. The rest of the liturgy is celebrated in response to that word. It is God's word that calls us to faith in baptism, to thanksgiving in Eucharist, to forgiveness in penance, to lasting fidelity in marriage, and so on. First we listen and receive from the Lord; only then can we respond.

So, too, the great prayers of blessing that stand at the center of many of our rites (Eucharistic Prayer, blessing of water, consecration of oil, etc.) all recall God's mighty wonders in the past and, on the basis of what God has already done, invoke God's blessing in the present. It is the experience of God's loving care in the past that gives us the courage to beg continued favor and the confidence to expect that God will fulfill the divine promises of eternal care and everlasting love now and in the future.

Another reflection of this principle appears in the sense of the liturgy as something given by God. We have at times oversimplified this insight and tried to claim divine authorship for every word and gesture in the liturgy. We recognize today that much of our worship is culturally derived, and thus open to change and variety. Yet there is still a sense of limit on this. The liturgy is not totally our own. We cannot create it from scratch, nor are we free to manipulate it at will to suit our purposes at a given moment. Even though our worship is our response to what God has done, our response itself is gift from the Lord. The liturgy is divinely inspired at the same time as it is humanly conditioned.

A Spirituality of Response

If this dynamic of God's initiative and our response is truly internalized, then it becomes the basis of a deep spirituality. Our spirituality is simply the way we respond to what God has done and is doing in our lives. From the very beginning, faith is a response. Grace precedes it, calls it forth, and makes it possible. And our growth into deeper faith is likewise a continuing series of responses, a constantly deepening "yes" to God's offer of love.

With this perspective, then, prayer is also response. We often think of prayer as our initiative, our asking God for help, our thanking God for favors received. But prayer is first of all a matter of listening. It is God who speaks first, God who touches us with love, God who brings us into the divine presence, God who invites us to share divine life, God who draws close to us. In true prayer, all we can really do is listen and then respond.

This may well be the reason why so many of us seem to have problems with prayer. We approach it as a task to be accomplished, a responsibility we must discharge, an initiative on our part to solicit God's response to us. Then prayer is evaluated in terms of what results it did or did not produce. Did God answer my prayer? Did I get what I asked for? Did God hear me? What a difference it makes when we begin to see prayer as our response to God! One who loves us calls to us, invites us to spend time together. Our challenge is simply to listen. "Be still, and know that I am God" (Ps 46:10, RSV). When we learn to recognize God's voice and to simply rest in God's presence, prayer becomes a joy and a gift rather than a burden and a duty. Of course, we must do more than rest. God will ask a response in action quite often. But this, too, is not burdensome, for it is an outgrowth of the love we have experienced. If we have drunk deeply of God's loving presence, we will find it a joy to respond to God's will in all things.

From Prayer to All of Life

In this way our prayer flows out into all of life. Our whole life becomes a response to God's initiative. God precedes us every step of the way along life's journey, constantly leading us on, calling us forward, inviting us to the next stage of our pilgrimage. The Christian life is a journey of continual conversion, and this conversion makes great demands upon us for change and growth. Yet conversion is really God's work in us, God-at-work in us, changing us, forming us, shaping us into the image of the Son. Our task is to let God have a free hand in making us new and then to live according to the new person that God has created, and continues to create, out of us.

To live life as a response to God's activity requires that we grow in constant awareness of God's presence in the daily events of our lives and especially in the people we meet on our way. God is always with us and just ahead of us. God works in and through the ordinary dynamics of our daily living, as well as in special times of prayer and worship. To live life in response to the divine presence also means that we must let go of control of our own lives and let God be in charge. That is probably the hardest part of this whole business of being Christian, for to let go requires great trust.

The story is told of a man who lost control of his car and went over a cliff. Thrown from the car, he managed to grab on to a branch of a small tree growing out of the cliff. Hanging suspended above a rock-strewn canyon, he saw no way to extricate himself from his precarious situation. Looking to the top of the cliff, he called out, "If anybody's up there, please help me!" There was no answer until he repeated the cry several times. Then a loud, booming voice answered, "Okay, I'll save you if you do what I tell you." "Anything you say, Lord," he answered, "anything!" "I only want one thing," the Lord said; "I want to know if you trust me." "Certainly," the man responded, "I trust you with all my heart." "Then," said God, "I want you to let go of that branch and I'll catch you." There was silence for a moment, and then the man cried out, "Is there anybody else up there?"

To really trust is difficult. We want to be in control, to have charge of our own lives. The American experience of freedom and pioneer individualism has formed us deeply, and we instinctively rebel against any threat to our autonomy. Yet spirituality demands a letting go, a surrender, a recognition of our utter dependence on God. Without God we can literally do nothing. We cannot move, eat, love, sleep, talk, or even exist without God's sustaining power and gift. Much less can we become holy on our own. The temptation to the heresy of Pelagius—thinking we can achieve salvation by our own power—is a constant one. The liturgy stands as a constant corrective to that tendency, for it continually reminds us that all we do is dependent on God's initiative.

This surrender of control also opens us to whatever

God may have in mind for us. If there is anything I have learned about this God of ours, it is that our God is a God of surprises. The mind of the Lord so far transcends our limited intellects that we can never fully comprehend what God wills. Every time I think I have it figured out, God has a new wrinkle in it. My plans are never quite the same as God's plans. So, paradoxical as it may seem, the predictable pattern of the liturgy with its stress on God's initiative prepares us to be surprised by the unpredictable mind of God.

Reflection Questions

1. Am I conscious of God's initiative in my own life? How has God called me, touched me, moved me?

2. Do I take enough time to reflect on my life in order to see there the hand of God? Have I learned to discern the Lord's direction of my daily life?

3. Do I really live my own life as a response to God's call? How have I responded to the Lord this day?

4. When we gather for the Eucharist, am I conscious of being part of a people called by God? Do I go to church because of that call from the Lord?

5. Does the proclamation of the Word and the Eucharistic Prayer lead me to give thanks for what God has done—in my life, for this community, in the world?

6. When I pray, do I take time just to listen for the Lord's word to me? Have I learned how to be still in God's presence and wait upon the Lord even if nothing seems to be happening?

7. How does my prayer influence the rest of my life? Can I name anything that has changed in my life lately because of my prayer? Do I let the Lord teach me how to live when I spend time in prayer?

8. How much do I trust in God? How far can I surrender control of my life to the Lord? Am I learning to let go more and more?

And Now, a Word from Our Sponsor

"BY THE WORD OF THE LORD the heavens were made; by the breath of his mouth all their host" (Psalm 33:6). God spoke, and there was light, and there were the earth and the sea, and there were the moon and the stars, and there were plants and animals, and there were humans. All things proceed from God's word.

This perspective on creation gives us some sense of how the people of Israel felt about the power of the spoken word. In our culture, which is heavily based on the print medium, we have not maintained such a lively sense of the spoken word. We "get it in writing" if we want to be certain about anything. The Hebrews depended more deeply upon the spoken word. This word causes things to happen. The Hebrews expressed this insight by their use of the same word (*dabar*) to stand for "word" and for "reality" or "event." The word is an event. The spoken word is powerful and effective, touching lives and changing history.

We know this to be true from our own experience, if we reflect on it a bit. The spoken word can frighten a person or cheer up one who is sad. It can move people to action or restrain them. It can depress or it can give hope. It can change the course of history and affect millions for better or for worse. The spoken word is indeed a word of power.

The Word of God

The power of the word is greatest when that word is of God. God's word creates and commands, compels and consoles. It is a powerful word that has its effect, a word that achieves God's will. Isaiah put it quite well:

> *For just as from the heavens*
> *the rain and snow come down*
> *And do not return there*
> *till they have watered the earth,*
> *making it fertile and fruitful,*
> *Giving seed to him who sows*
> *and bread to him who eats,*
> *So shall my word be*
> *that goes forth from my mouth;*
> *It shall not return to me void,*
> *but shall do my will,*
> *achieving the end for which I sent it.*
> (Isaiah 55:10-11)

The word of God as an event appears most fully with the coming of Jesus, the Incarnate Word. "God . . . last of all in these days has spoken to us by his Son" (Hebrews 1:1-2). It is the presence of Jesus in our midst that gives the fullest potential to the proclamation of the word in the liturgical assembly. As the Second Vatican Council declared, "He is present in his word, since it is he himself who speaks when the holy scriptures are read in the Church" (Constitution on the Sacred Liturgy, no. 7).

Henry Ward Beecher was once asked what he would do if he were sitting in a church and someone next to him fell asleep. His reply was that he would send some-

one up to the pulpit to awaken the preacher! If the
preaching is boring, the word of God is not really being
proclaimed. The word proclaimed in the assembly is a
word of power, bearing all the potential invested in it
when God first spoke that word. When the written
word of Scripture is proclaimed publicly, it comes to
life again and is "enfleshed" in the voice of the reader.
The spoken word thus has a power that transcends the
word in its printed form. It is for this reason that the
Church has always attached a special importance to the
proclamation of the word in the assembly, over and
above the value of reading the Scriptures in private.
The word proclaimed possesses an immediacy and an
urgency. It confronts the hearers and demands a
response. If the word is really heard, it changes the
hearers and affects the whole of life. Such an experience
is clearly an event in the full sense of the Hebrew
dabar.

It is important to note that this public proclamation
of the word requires a communal setting. Even if the
group is very small, it is necessary to have both a pro-
claimer and a hearer. Thus the word reaches its fullest
potential in the assembly, and this truth leads to some
valuable insights into the proper use of the Scriptures.

Devotional Bible Reading

The liturgical use of the Bible certainly indicates that
the word of God is meant to guide our whole lives. As
with everything in the liturgy, it transcends the time of
worship and points us toward a life based on the word.
Far from being in competition, the public proclamation
and the private reading of the Scriptures should support
and complement one another.

For centuries Catholics and Protestants have debated the proper use of the Scriptures. The Catholic tradition has insisted that the Bible is only properly interpreted by the Church, which was too often identified with the hierarchy alone. Against this, the Reformers insisted that each person has the power to interpret the Scriptures privately under the power of the Spirit.

The liturgy suggests a possible ecumenical meeting point from which a solution to the dilemma might be developed. The liturgy insists that the word is meant to be proclaimed and heard; it is in this shared experience of the word that its full potential is unleashed. Thus this communal experience of the word should stand as the touchstone against which to test any and all private interpretations. I suspect that this is the fundamental truth that the Catholic position has tried to protect, but it is only in the current age, with its recovery of the full sense of the local Church, that the phrase "interpreted by the Church" could be seen in this wider context. There is clearly a value to personal Scripture reading, and there is room for personal interpretation and application of the word to daily life. But when the personal interpretation and the understanding of the community come into conflict, then the communal experience holds priority. Ultimately, of course, even the particular community's interpretation must be in accord with the universal understanding of the Church, but the communal experience of the word is a vital safeguard against inadequate understanding of the Scriptures.

A Common Search

It seems to me that a full appreciation of the importance of the communal setting for the proper interpretation of the word of God suggests some wider implications for our daily living. Does it not imply that the search for truth should always be a common search? Various commentators have pointed out a contemporary trend that can be called a "privatizing of truth." Along with what many see as an overemphasis on the values of pluralism, our society has undergone a progressive breakdown in social cohesion. Much of this breakdown is a result of the loss of any common value system. In our concern to safeguard individual freedom, we have been tempted to conclude that any opinion is valid and any position is tenable, no matter how unreasonable or how destructive to society.

Some of this process has undoubtedly been fostered by the rapid development in recent years in the communications field. The proliferation of the electronic media has provided a forum for the dissemination of the ideas of anyone who can create enough of a sensation to get on the evening newscast. Someone once noted that ideas become respectable just by being talked about. Hence, the reporting of even outlandish positions tends to make them appear respectable and tenable.

The more recent development of cable systems portends an even greater degree of fragmentation. The rapid expansion of channels for communication that cable affords enables the development of "narrowcasting," that is, the airing of programs targeted to a specific small audience. This can be a real boon to those with specialized tastes and to various groups, including churches, with special educational needs. But it can also lead to even less of a common fund of ideas and experiences on which to base social interaction. Ironically, too many channels of communication can lead to a breakdown of communication on a social level. If you've ever had trouble finding someone who watched the same movie on television that you watched last night, you have experienced the tip of this iceberg.

It is no easy task to find the proper balance between individual freedom and pluralism and society's need for common values. It is clear to most people that a return to a simple authoritarian insistence on older values is a dead-end street. If we are to come to a common sense of values, it will have to be through dialogue and a gradually emerging consensus. Our communal experience of sharing the word of God in our search for ultimate truth might well teach us the importance of a common endeavor in all searching for truth. Obviously, simply attending worship services will not automatically lead us to a commitment to search for truth together, but if we let the experience of worship penetrate deeper and deeper into our lives, it may lead us in the right direction.

Reflection Questions

1. How good am I as a listener? Do I listen attentively to each word spoken to me by a friend?

2. How carefully do I listen to the word of God proclaimed in the liturgy?

3. What reading or homily can I remember that really moved me when I heard it proclaimed? Why did that particular word affect me so deeply? What effect did it have on my daily life?

4. Is the reading of Scripture an important part of my spirituality? Do I need to set aside time on a more regular basis to read and ponder the word of the Lord?

5. Would a Bible study group help me to probe God's word more fruitfully? Can I think of instances when the insight of someone else helped me correct my understanding of Scripture?

6. How do I go about forming my opinion on issues of importance? Where do I look for guidance in finding the truth? Am I open to the insights and opinions of others? Am I willing to test my own insights, even on personal matters, by asking others to critique my position?

7. What role does the church community play in my decisions about what is right and wrong and what is God's will today?

Getting It All Together

FROM THE ORIENT comes the story of a man who was granted an opportunity to see both heaven and hell. When he arrived at hell, he found everyone seated at a huge banquet table piled high with all kinds of delectable foods. The diners were trying to eat, but the chopsticks were all six feet long! Try as they might, they could not get the food into their mouths, and so they were filled with frustration.

Going to heaven, the man expected a far different situation; but when he arrived, he found a nearly identical arrangement. Another overflowing banquet table filled the hall, and each diner was equipped with six-foot-long chopsticks. But these diners were filled with joy because they were all feeding the people across from them!

There is no room for rugged individualism in heaven, nor is there room for it in the Church on earth. We have seen that we are called to be listeners because God speaks to us. We are called to listen together because God speaks to us together. One of the most basic facts about God's dealings with humanity is that God calls us as a people. Our God is a God who called, shaped, and worked through a chosen people.

This pattern is clear in the Old Testament, for whenever God called an individual, it was really a covenant with a whole people that was envisioned. It was so with Noah; it was so with Abraham, Isaac, and Jacob; it was so with Moses; it was so with Isaiah and with all the prophets. God always seems to be busy either establishing or renewing the covenant with the chosen people of Israel.

Corporate Identity

The Israelites had a very lively sense of God's community-minded approach to salvation. Scripture scholars speak of Israel as having a strong sense of "corporate personality," which simply means that they saw the whole people as somehow gathered together and represented by the person of the king or leader or prophet. So what God said to the king affected everybody, and the king's response to God was Israel's response.

We have some sense of this in our own culture, for we allow the president of the country to speak for the whole nation in many areas. And we recognize the queen of England as somehow embodying the whole of the British national identity. But it seems that this was both deeper and more comprehensive for the people of the Old Testament. We Americans tend to insist more deeply on the rights and freedom of each individual, especially in the area of religion. In this area, which was central for Israel's corporate identity, we seldom think of allowing any one person to speak for all of us. Even less would we assume that our salvation or God's approach to us depended on the actions of another, even if that other person is the president or the pope.

We have learned well Ezekiel's insistence that the old proverb about the father's sour grapes setting his children's teeth on edge should be spoken no more, for God judges each person according to his or her life (Ezekiel 18:2-3).

American Individualism

Yet I suspect that we are influenced less by Ezekiel than by the radical individualism of the Enlightenment thinkers. The Enlightenment in eighteenth-century Europe provided many of the fundamental beliefs of the founding fathers of this country. This resulted in a form of government that was soundly based on the rights of the individual, a government limited by legal and constitutional safeguards to protect those rights. This is clearly a valuable result of the Enlightenment's stress on the individual. But our subsequent history has shaped us, too, and much of that history has been dominated by the vision of the frontier, always there, always offering a new beginning for the pioneer who got nervous when an area got too settled and didn't leave enough "elbowroom." The mythic characters we idolize tend to be loners, independent, "self-made men" who lean on nobody and defy the forces of nature or of evil alone. The lone cowpoke, the mountain man, the prospector, the heroic pioneer, the homesteader, the Lone Ranger, and even the outlaw disappear over the horizon or ride off into the sunset over and over again. Even our political language and current national endeavors betray the abiding power of these images. Since we no longer have a physical frontier to conquer in the West, we tackle the social problems of the "New Frontier," and we challenge outer space as the remaining unconquered frontier.

These new frontiers, however, are a bit different, and conquering them requires more cooperative effort. No space flight is achieved by a single individual, and no social problems will be remedied without a great deal of cooperation. The days of the rugged individual are numbered, though we have not fully accepted that fact yet as a society.

This tradition of hyper-individualism is very different from the long tradition of the Church. Some wag has said that God so loved the world that God didn't send a committee. But when Jesus began his ministry, he quickly began to gather disciples around him, and this group of disciples became the nucleus of the Church. As we noted in the last chapter, the very name for "church" in Greek, *ekklesia,* means those called out and called together. The Church is the new people of God in the New Testament, and to be the Church is to be a community of believers. In the Christian perspective, there is no *really* individual salvation. Even as a child, I was taught that you can't get to heaven alone; you have to help others on the way. It is significant to note that the word "saint" is almost never used in the New Testament except in the plural. God deals with us as a people, and our salvation is worked out in, through, and with other people. God's grace is available to us, but it involves the ones beside us.

This goes against the grain for many people today because they have really adopted the individualistic approach. This is true even in the Church, and perhaps *especially* in the Church. For many, many people, religion is primarily or even solely a private matter, a

relationship "between me and my God." To recognize
Christianity as fundamentally other-oriented and
community-based demands quite a revolution in the
minds of many.

Communal Prayer

The problem of individualism shows up in one of
the most subtle but most pervasive difficulties in our
worship today—understanding true communal prayer.
Communal prayer is quite different from having five
hundred people praying in the same place at the same
time. That can be, and often is, simply five hundred individual prayers rather than one communal prayer. Yet
liturgy is definitely intended to be one unified prayer of
a community praying as a community. Part of the
problem, of course, is that many of our worship
assemblies are not really communities in any significant
sense of the term. But part of the problem is also that
we are so used to seeing prayer as a private matter that
many of us would not recognize a truly communal
prayer if we were caught in the middle of one.

The liturgy has much to teach us here, and what it
has to teach is basic for Christian spirituality. The
liturgy takes very seriously the ancient doctrine that the
Church is the body of Christ. We really are one body,
united by the very lifeblood of Christ that sustains us,
living by the one Spirit that dwells within us and binds
us together. Therefore, when we gather for prayer, we
pray as one body in one Spirit. So many people have
complained that the revised liturgy doesn't allow
enough time for prayer, as if the liturgy itself is not
prayer. Sadly, this is really how many people see the
liturgy—not as prayer itself but as an obstacle to

prayer, since prayer is seen as a private communication between God and the individual. The celebration of the liturgy may well need more space and less filler, more silence and less talking, but not so that we can "pray for a change." All of the liturgy is prayer: hymns and responses, proclamations and silences, gestures and processions. But it is clearly communal prayer, not private prayer.

In a wider sense the liturgy points us toward the realization that in the Christian scheme of things, there is really no such thing as "private" prayer. We never cease to be the body of Christ, and so our prayer is never really prayer in isolation. Whenever we pray, we pray as members of the body, in union with all the other members of the Church. Perhaps if we had a more vital sense of this communal dimension to all prayer, we would more easily perceive the liturgy as the gathering of our prayer into one at the summit of the Church's life. Perhaps, too, a clear sense of our unity in the body whenever we pray would help us cope more easily with those times when prayer is hard, those dry times in our lives when we could use the support of others in prayer. That support is always available to us, for we are never really alone when we pray.

Being One Body

Spirituality, we have said, goes far beyond the times we spend in worship and at prayer. So, too, this sense of being one body extends to many dimensions of our life in the world. The liturgy can lead us to a strong sense of responsibility for others. We really do belong to one another. The answer to Cain's question is "yes"—

we are our brother's and our sister's keeper, and the liturgy knows this. In the General Intercessions, or Prayer of the Faithful, we properly pray for those who have special needs. We pray for the common needs of the local community and the area in which we live. We are also invited to pray for national concerns and to reach out even further to worldwide needs, both civil and religious. Like the proverbial pebble in the pond, the liturgy challenges our concern to grow in ever-widening circles.

By our concern and active love for others, we carry on the work of building up the family of God. This requires a number of basic attitudes that are important in our spiritual growth. It requires, first of all, a deep respect for persons, a recognition that every other person is loved by God and can be a channel of God's grace in the world. The liturgy presumes such respect, based on the innate value of that person in God's sight, not on material success, political power, or any other criterion of importance. James insists that such surface distinctions have no place in the assembly (James 2:1-9). When we gather for worship, we must leave all such claims to status and power outside, for they have no place before the table of the Lord.

Building up the body of Christ also requires an honest respect for differences. One wit has said that the world is divided into people who think they are right! When we view our position and perspective as the only possible one, when we insist that we have a corner on the truth, we foster division. It is only people who accept differences as normal and healthy who can really bring a community together. It is simply part of true respect for persons to respect their right to their own views and insights, and to value the creative interaction such differences can generate.

To live with differences and still be a community, though, it is necessary to grow in genuine love. There will always be tensions in a real community; only a totalitarian system can ensure perfect harmony, and that is only an apparent harmony. A Christmas card I once received put it well. It read simply: "If we have love in our hearts, disagreement will do us no harm; if we do not have love in our hearts, agreement will do us no good."

To truly love is to put others first, to consider their needs before our own. Most of us have a sense of how this can transform human relationships. But it could also transform whole societies. Peter Maurin, co-founder with Dorothy Day of the Catholic Worker movement, once wrote an intriguing little piece that tickles our imaginations as to how things could be. He called it "A Case for Utopia":

> *The world would be better off*
> *if people tried to become better,*
> *and people would become better*
> *if they stopped trying to become better off.*
> *For when everyone tries to become better off,*
> *nobody is better off.*
> *But when everyone tries to become better*
> *everybody is better off.*
> *Everyone would be rich*
> *if nobody tried to become richer,*
> *and nobody would be poor*
> *if everybody tried to be the poorest.*
> *And everybody would be what he ought to be*
> *if everybody tried to be*
> *what he wants the other fellow to be.* *

*Reprinted in "Easy Essays," *The Catholic Worker* 49, no. 1 (May 1982) 6.

The liturgy celebrates the covenant that God has made with us, and it calls us continually to renew that covenant and to recognize ourselves as one people of the covenant. But it must always go further than that. The Hasidic Jews note that the Talmud says that the stork is called the devout or loving one because it gives so much love to its mate and its young. But they wondered why the stork is classed in the Scriptures among the unclean birds; they answered that it was because the stork gives love only to its own. It must not be so among the followers of Jesus. The covenant that God has made with us is a covenant meant for all peoples. God has called us for the sake of others, and our concern must reach to the ends of the earth—and perhaps beyond.

Reflection Questions

1. How community-minded am I? Do I see my own individuality in the context of relationships with others?

2. What are the important communities in my life? With what groups do I identify?

3. Do I find myself often insisting on my own rights as if others had no claim on me? How much am I influenced by the "Lone Ranger" mentality?

4. Has my religion been a private matter "between me and Jesus"? Do I agree that Christianity is "fundamentally other-oriented and community-based"?

5. How much do I experience the liturgy as truly communal prayer, as a prayer offered by all of the assembly as one body?

6. Do I experience the hymns and responses as prayer? Why or why not?

7. When I pray in private, am I conscious of my brothers and sisters who are always with me? Is my prayer always in and for the body of Christ?

8. Do I carry that sense of being part of the body of Christ throughout my day? What difference does it make in my life?

9. Do I accept differences and disagreements as normal in the life of a community? Is my love strong enough to keep differences from becoming divisions?

10. How wide is my concern? How far does my love for others reach?

An Attitude of Gratitude

SHORT POEM: "How odd / Of God / To choose / The Jews" (W. N. Ewer). But choose them God did. And perhaps they thought it odd of God, too. At any rate, they were very aware of all that God had done for them in making them a chosen people, and so they were easily inclined to prayers of praise and gratitude.

GRAFFITO: "Mary was a Jewish mother!" And so she was, and her son was Jewish, too. It is a great shock to many Christians when they realize that Jesus was Jewish. It's always a bit awkward when the object of one's devotion turns out to be one of those people against whom one has been prejudiced. Jesus was a Jew, and so he prayed as a Jew. The apostles were also all Jewish; the womb from which the Church was born was a Jewish one. It is only natural, therefore, that the Church's style and pattern of worship have deep Jewish roots.

Berakah

The common Jewish prayer response to God's blessings was a prayer of blessing known as *berakah* (plural: *berakoth*). The word "blessing" here, however, has a bit different meaning than that commonly associated with the word in our culture. When we speak of blessing, we tend to think first of a blessing *of* something; but for the Jews, the primary meaning was a blessing *for* something. In this form of prayer, one blesses God *for* creation, *for* redemption, *for* whatever gift God has given. To bless in this sense is often translated in English as "to praise" and "to thank."

Such blessing prayers were common among the Jews, both in formal worship and in ordinary life. Scholars have described two main types of *berakoth*, the spontaneous and the formal. In the spontaneous form, there are two parts: a brief expression of blessing God or the name of God, often very stylized, and then an expression of the motive or reason for which God is being thanked and praised. Various examples of such blessing prayers can be found in the Bible, as in Genesis 24:26-27, when Abraham's servant finds a wife for Isaac in a providential if not miraculous way. The servant bows in worship and says: "Blessed be the Lord, the God of my master Abraham, who has not let his constant kindness toward my master fail. As for myself also, the Lord has led me straight to the house of my master's brother." The structure is obvious: a blessing and the reason for it. The prayer is simple and straightforward, yet rich and beautiful. In the Gospels, too, we find such prayers; Jesus himself prayed: "I offer you praise, O Father, Lord of heaven and earth, because what you have hidden from the learned and the clever you have revealed to the merest children" (Luke 10:21). Other examples in the Scriptures can be found in Exodus 18:9-10, Matthew 11:25, and John 11:41-42.

The formal or cultic *berakah* also begins with an expression of blessing, followed by the statement of the motive, but here the motive is expanded and recalls, often in great detail, the wondrous works of God on Israel's behalf throughout the centuries. Sometimes this second section would lead into prayers of petition that God would continue to be generous with divine blessings. The *berakah* would then conclude with a brief final blessing, often in the form of a doxology. Examples of formal *berakoth* can be found in Psalms 103 and 104 and in Ephesians 1:3–3:21.

The Eucharistic Prayer

It is this formal or liturgical type of *berakah* that is commonly seen as the ancestor of the Christian Eucharistic Prayer. This central prayer of the Eucharist begins with a rather stylized set of responses at the beginning of the Preface ("Let us give thanks to the Lord our God—It is right to give him thanks and praise"), followed by a recalling of God's marvelous works. Then a series of prayers of petition is concluded with a doxology of praise ("Through him, with him, in him, in the unity of the Holy Spirit, all glory and honor is yours, almighty Father, for ever and ever"). The recital of the narrative of the Last Supper is really part of the recital of God's wondrous works. The fourth Eucharistic Prayer in the Roman Catholic tradition offers one of the clearest examples of this *berakah* structure, but all the Eucharistic Prayers contain the same basic elements.

I have spent some time on this prayer form because it is a central pattern in our worship tradition. It is also a very helpful pattern to use in personal prayer. I was once told that a good Orthodox Jew is expected to recite at least one hundred *berakoth* per day—upon awakening, for example: "Blessed are you, Lord our God, for you have given us another day to live"; while washing up in the morning: "Blessed are you, Lord of all creation, for you have given us water to cleanse and refresh us"; before eating: "Blessed be the Lord of all things, who has given us this bread to eat and this wine to drink." And so on throughout the day the faithful Jew constantly gives thanks for all the favors God bestows on the world.

A Thankful Life

Such a pattern of prayer, for the Jew or for the Christian, seems to lead almost inevitably to a basic attitude of gratitude woven into the fabric of one's life. Even the regular celebration of the Eucharistic Prayer should lead the worshiper to such an approach to life. Conversely, this basic attitude, if lived on a day-to-day basis, would certainly bring more meaning to the celebration of the Eucharist itself. It would be a very commendable practice for Christians to strive to make the *berakah* an integral part of their daily lives. Since Christian spirituality is a spirituality of response to God's initiative, gratitude is one of the most fundamental emotions of the Christian life.

Such a sense of thankfulness would also lead us to a healthy respect and care for all of God's creation. To recognize all things as gifts from the Lord is to recognize their inherent value and also their ability to speak to us of God's love for us. Such an attitude would surely lead us to treat nature and all created things with more respect than our recent past evidences. The rape of the land, pollution, waste, and litter all witness to an ungrateful attitude toward God's gifts.

An attitude of gratitude would also lead to a real concern for justice for all people, especially in the distribution of the goods of the earth. Part of respecting creation involves recognizing the limits of creation. And in the context of a limited creation, we recognize the necessity of using only that portion of God's gifts that we really need for our lives. To use more than our share is to deprive others of what they need for their very sustenance. To be grateful is not to be greedy.

If we are really grateful, we recognize our dependence on God and our interdependence on others. We are not masters of creation but its stewards. We do not own God's gifts, but they are given for our use to the extent that we really need them. Much of the injustice that afflicts so many of the world's inhabitants is a result of poor distribution, not actual shortage. It is generally agreed, for example, that we currently produce enough food in the world to feed everybody, but because of waste and inefficient distribution, millions go to bed hungry each night. When we realize that what we have is a gift, and not ours by right, we will be more willing to share what we have been given.

The Power of Symbols

Another aspect of respect for creation involves letting created things speak to us. The liturgy relies heavily on symbols to communicate God's presence and message to us. Symbols speak to us on many levels of consciousness (and even on unconscious levels). Symbols can touch our emotions as well as our intellects; they can convey a deep sense of meaning as well as information; they can embody a presence as well as an idea. We Americans are not overly aware of the power of symbols. We tend to think of the symbolic as the unreal and, therefore, the unimportant. Yet symbols bring us in touch with reality, often with a deeper sense of reality than our daily productive activity. Symbolic activity enters into the realm of the poetic, and this means that we have to learn (or relearn) how to let it speak to us.

If we do learn to enter into the realm of the symbolic in worship, we may also be led to be more open to what all of reality has to say to us. We rush through life so rapidly at times that we don't really see what is around us. The liturgy invites us to a more contemplative approach to life, an approach of wonder. We need to learn to really see water and listen to its sounds in a brook or a fountain and feel it running cool over our hand or our tired feet and taste its quenching freshness. G. K. Chesterton once suggested that we would perhaps better appreciate the marvel of water in our rivers and streams if all at once it turned to wine and we had no more water.

To really appreciate water or light or earth or oil or any part of creation is to let it speak to us. The more we learn to probe beneath the surface of things, the more we will discover there what the poet Gerard Manley Hopkins called "the dearest freshness deep down things." And the more we discover this depth, the more we will delight in the symbols of the liturgy— the bread and wine, the light and oil, the words and gestures, the meals and washings, the touches and embraces that the liturgy uses to express and celebrate God's actions and God's presence in our midst.

As we come to appreciate God's gifts, we find ourselves in a circle, for to be grateful is to be filled with wonder, and to be filled with wonder is to be led to give thanks and praise to the One who is the source and sustainer of all that is.

Reflection Questions

1. Is the Jesus I know Jewish? Does it disturb my usual image of him to realize that he was a Jew all his life on earth?

2. Do I ever give thanks to God for the heritage we have received from our Jewish brothers and sisters? Do I see Jews today as God's chosen people?

3. Could the *berakah* form of prayer be helpful for my own daily prayer?

4. How much do I live with an attitude of gratitude for all the Lord gives me each day? Do I need, perhaps, to "count my blessings" more often?

5. When I come to Eucharist, do I come ready to give thanks because I have been mindful of God's gifts all week?

6. In what ways can I express my gratitude to God?

7. Is a concern for justice an important part of my spirituality? Does this flow from my experience of prayer and worship?

8. Do I live with a sense of wonder? Do I take time to smell the flowers and let them speak to me of God? Have I ever really taken time to appreciate water or bread or wine or oil?

For Those Who Know How to See

LITTLE JOHNNY was new to the parochial school, but he was already beginning to figure out that his teacher was very good at finding ways to relate religion to every subject. One day in class, Sister asked the children, "What is small and gray, has a big, bushy tail, and feeds on nuts?" Johnny raised his hand, and when the teacher called on him, he answered, "Sister, my head tells me it's a squirrel, but my heart tells me it's the Lord Jesus."

An Incarnational Faith

Johnny was carrying things just a bit too far, but he had figured out the basic meaning of the Incarnation, one of the most fundamental doctrines of the Christian creed. The Incarnation refers primarily to the Son of God becoming a human being and living among us. But the doctrine encompasses more than Jesus alone, for from its earliest centuries the Church has seen in Jesus the uniting of the divine with all humanity. In addition, the Church has recognized that the infinite God can be found in all of finite creation, that God's presence may be discovered in the ordinary things and people in our lives.

49

The effect of this belief on Christian worship and spirituality has varied in direct relationship to the view of Christ that Christians have held in any historical period. The overemphasis on the divinity of Jesus that resulted from the Arian denial of that divinity, a conflict that lasted for centuries, led to a near eclipse of this incarnational principle. Not only was Christ himself seen more and more as the almighty Lord and less and less as truly one of us, but Christians also began to see the things and people necessary for worship as sacred, untouchable, and radically different from the ordinary things of life. In popular piety, at least, God was to be found only in sacred spaces; God acted only in sacred rites; God was mediated only through sacred people, the clergy and religious.

In recent times, both biblical scholars and theologians have been helping us recognize more fully the human side of Jesus, to see him as truly "like us in all things but sin" (Eucharistic Prayer IV). Jesus is fully divine, truly God, yet he is also fully human, truly like us. As with every swing of a pendulum, there may be some danger of an overemphasis on the humanity of Jesus now to the exclusion of his divinity, but I suspect that we have a long way to go before most people adequately recognize the human side of Christ.

An Incarnate Worship

The more deeply we appreciate the interpenetration of the divine and the human in Jesus, the more we will understand the liturgy's rich use of created things and human acts. The liturgy stands as a constant corrective to the tendency to overspiritualize religion, to shun the human and the created as unworthy, sinful, or inher-

ently evil. Though there have been numerous move-
ments in that direction throughout the Church's history,
the liturgy has never fully succumbed to that temptation.

The temptation is not just an ancient one, however,
but manifests itself quite often in our own day. Many
people view worship as something that should be separate from ordinary life, and so they have trouble ac-
cepting the use of ordinary things in worship and the
ministry of ordinary (that is, non-ordained) people in
liturgy. They have been disturbed by the introduction
of contemporary styles of music and instruments in
worship, by the ministry of lay distributors of communion, by communion in the hand, by the use of bread
that looks and tastes like bread, by every attempt to
bring the things of ordinary life into worship. And
these people are quite right in their basic instinct. They
sense, perhaps subconsciously, that these changes are
not merely cosmetic.

What has changed is not just the externals of the
liturgy, but the underlying perception of how God
works in our lives. From a perspective that focused
primarily on God as intervening in life in extraordinary
ways, and therefore being found most often in extraordinary (sacred) times and places, the liturgy has shifted
to a more incarnational stance that looks for God in the
ordinary, because it sees God as intimately present in
all of creation and at work in all times and places. The
older view relied very much on the dichotomy between
the sacred and the profane, between the spiritual and
the material, between the holy and the unholy. The
current stance recaptures the fundamental insight that
for the Christian there can be no sacred/profane

dichotomy, for in Christ the spiritual and the material are so fully united that they cannot be separated again. As the theologian Pierre Teilhard de Chardin put it, "Nothing is profane for those who know how to see."

Immanence and Transcendence

What is at issue here is the balance between the immanence and the transcendence of God. God is totally Other, transcending the limits of our world and the capabilities of our minds to comprehend. Yet God is also immanent, present everywhere and in everything, closer to us than we are to ourselves. To focus too much on the transcendent is to miss God's presence all around us; to focus too much on the immanent is to make our God too small, to forget that God really is God. To maintain the balance is a constant challenge.

In the liturgy this challenge includes the question of the proper degree of enculturation in worship. How much of our culture should be part of the liturgy? In what ways should our worship be influenced by the events, the styles, the language, and the customs of our society? There are no simple answers to such questions. The word of God is a two-edged sword, and it confronts every culture with a dual thrust: it will affirm and support and raise up whatever is good in the culture, and it will condemn and reject and destroy whatever is evil. So, too, the liturgy will incorporate into itself whatever is in harmony with the Christian message, but it must also reject and stand in judgment against whatever in the culture is opposed to the gospel. It takes careful reflection and a sensitive heart to discern what can be accepted and what must be rejected. Underlying the process must be a deep apprecia-

tion of the Incarnation, a solid acceptance of the fact
that God has chosen to work through the human and
the created as well as in extraordinary ways.

An Incarnational Spirituality

The liturgy's recovery of this incarnational principle
ought to lead to a recovery of the same principle in our
personal spirituality. A liturgical spirituality will be
marked by a certain rootedness and earthiness. For too
long spirituality has been seen as a matter of escaping
our humanity and becoming angelic. An incarnational
spirituality does not disdain the limited and the created,
but it seeks to embrace it more deeply, finding God,
not in escaping from the material, but rather in probing
more deeply into its depths.

These really are two radically different approaches
to the spiritual life. The religions of the Far East tend to
adopt the spiritualizing principle and see creation as
evil, or at least as a basic hindrance to union with God.
Those who hold this view seek to become holy precisely by escaping the material world, by becoming
otherworldly. The Christian impulse should be just the
opposite. In light of the Incarnation, the Christian seeks
God in and through the limited and the material. Looking deeply into every person and every thing, the Christian seeks to find there the God who is at the root of
all reality. Even more, in the human person the Christian expects to see the face of Christ, the God-Man who
has forever united the divine and the human.

Just as there is a tension in theology between God's
immanence and God's transcendence, just as there is a
tension in the liturgy between enculturation and the experience of the Other, so in our spirituality there needs

to be a tension between the virtue of detachment and the need to value and find God in creation. The gospel is clear that we must be ready to surrender all things for the sake of the kingdom, be willing to let go of whatever stands between us and God, be free of any attachments that keep us from following Jesus. Detachment is a fundamental Christian virtue. Yet it is also clear from the example of Jesus, as well as from the basic fact of the Incarnation itself, that we are not to disdain God's creation or the people God has placed in our lives.

To Wonder

Perhaps the key to a proper balance here can be found in the quality of wonder we mentioned in the last chapter. The capacity for wonder is often underdeveloped in our culture because we are so pragmatic and production-oriented. To stand in wonder before another person or thing is to see it deeply and to appreciate it for its richness. It is to see it ultimately as revelatory, as capable of revealing God to us. If we learn to value and to use all the created things available to us with a sense of wonder, we may be less tempted to grasp them and become attached to them as if they really belonged to us, while at the same time we may be able to truly let them speak to us of God. So, too, we can truly love the people God gives us to love and allow them to reveal God's love to us without becoming possessive and inordinately attached to them. It is a question of seeing the mystery that lies at the center of all things and of every person. We are always drawn to mystery, but instinctively we know that we cannot possess it or claim it as ours by right. We stand before the mystery in awe and wonder, but we remain open to the possibility that God may choose to reveal the divine presence to us in another way or in another person tomorrow, so we must always be ready to let go and move on.

Another area where an incarnational spirituality can be helpful is in the proper appreciation of the human body. Most of us are still deeply affected by the Manichean view of the body as evil, as a prison of the soul from which we need to escape to be holy. The Incarnation proclaims that the human person, body and soul, is called to holiness. If the body were inherently evil, the Son of God could not have taken on flesh and become human. To be human is to be embodied. We do not really exist as a separate body and soul, only temporarily united. The human person is an embodied spirit. We are radically, not just accidentally, bodily in our nature. An incarnational spirituality, therefore, must involve a deep integration of the self, an integration that recognizes and deepens the interpenetration of the spiritual and the bodily within us.

The Body at Worship

An uncomfortableness with the body is evident in most liturgical assemblies today. By and large, we are not very open yet to the use of dance and movement or to the richness of gesture and touch in our worship. The liturgy itself calls for a good bit of ritual gesture and often uses physical contact to communicate God's action (imposition of hands, sign of peace, etc.). The liturgy is also open to sensitive use of movement and even dance to express our response to the Lord. There is need in our worship for a much richer use of gesture, but our discomfort inclines us to restrict most ritual gestures to the presider alone. We have much to learn yet about the liturgy as the action of all the gathered assembly.

As we grow more comfortable with the use of the body in worship, we should also find ourselves more aware of the role that our bodies can have in all of our prayer. What we do with our bodies during prayer can have a very deep impact on the quality and tone of our prayer. Sometimes we find the body to be just an obstacle to prayer, and we suspect that we could pray better if we could be rid of the body for a while. But we must pray as humans, not as angels, and so we must pray with our bodies and not just with our minds. Note that I said *with* our bodies, not in spite of our bodies. The body can be a very powerful aid to prayer. If you wish to try a simple experience of the potential of the body in prayer, try slowly reciting the Lord's Prayer in each of the following bodily positions: standing with arms at your sides, sitting on a chair, sitting cross-legged on the floor, kneeling with hands folded, lying on your stomach, lying on your back, lying on your side in a fetal position, standing on tiptoe reaching skyward, and whatever other position you can comfortably assume. Even though it is the same prayer being recited over and over, the tone and thus the meaning the prayer takes on will vary, depending on what past feelings and memories each position evokes.

If our worship and our prayer experiences lead us to a deeper respect for, and appreciation of, the human body, we should also expect this to have an effect on the way we deal with the body in daily life. Christians have frequently lamented our society's casual attitude toward sexuality and its preoccupation with sexual pleasure. There is no doubt that our society has a distorted and unhealthy approach to sex. But is it not possible that the negative attitude that many Christians have toward the body and sex is intimately related to our society's confusion? Is it not possible that the overemphasis on sexuality today is at least in part a reaction to the rejection of the body in the name of Christianity in past eras? And even more deeply, is not the current societal approach to sex just another expression of a lack of true respect for the human body?

In any case, it seems to me that an incarnational spirituality offers us the basis for a healthy and holy view of the body and of sexuality. A deep sense of wonder, an appreciation of the mystery involved in the way we are made, can lead us to a true respect for, and proper valuing of, the body and sex. They are not the center and focus of our lives. Only God deserves that place, and the mystery of God's presence must be constantly sought and reverenced. But neither do we disdain the body or sexuality, for they can be deeply revelatory. They can be precisely the place where God's presence can be seen and felt and reverenced.

Reflection Questions

1. What is my image of Jesus? Is he fully divine for me? Is he fully human?

2. How comfortable am I worshiping with ordinary things and ordinary people?

3. Do I find God in the ordinary things and people in my life? What was the last thing that spoke to me of God's presence? What made it transparent for me?

4. Is my spirituality an incarnate one? Is it integrated into my life, encompassing my whole person and all my activities?

5. What role does my body play in my relationship with the Lord? Have I learned to pray comfortably with my body? What bodily positions do I find most conducive to prayer?

6. Do I ever thank the Lord for the gift of my body? Can I praise God with my body? How?

7. Do I view my sexuality as a gift of God? Have I ever experienced God's presence through my sexuality? Is my approach to sex one of reverence for the mystery of life and love?

Where Heaven and Earth Meet

THE STORY IS TOLD that Moses was met by a group of Hebrews when he came back down the mountain the second time, after the first tablets of the commandments had been broken. When he got near enough, they asked him how it went this time. "Not too well," he replied. "It was tough bargaining. We get the milk and honey, but the anti-adultery clause stays!"

Some encounters with God don't go quite as we expect or hope. But the ultimate purpose of all forms of worship and the point of all spirituality is to lead us to an encounter with God, to foster the experience of the divine. Adherents of various religions have often spoken of such experiences as taking place where heaven and earth meet, at the boundary between the two, in that "no man's land" which doesn't totally belong to either realm. This language can be problematic if it seems to assume the kind of separation between the realms of the divine and the human that contradicts the Incarnation.

Recent scholarship by anthropologists, however, has opened up a very fertile area for our understanding of worship and of spirituality. This research has focused on rites of passage in various societies, and especially on the liminal stage of these rituals. Rites of passage include puberty rites, marriage rituals, and a variety of other forms of celebration that involve a transition from one social role or position to another. The basic pattern of such rites was described near the turn of the century by Arnold van Gennep. All rites of passage involve three main stages: a separation from the group or tribe or family, which involves a separation from the previous social position; a marginal or liminal (Latin: *limen* = threshold) stage, which is "betwixt and between"; and finally a reaggregation or re-entrance into the social structure of the group in a new social role.

Many Americans first saw a rite of passage depicted in the television mini-series based on Alex Haley's *Roots.* An early segment of the series followed Kunta Kinte as he experienced the puberty rites of his African tribe. Separated for a time from the rest of the village, he and his companions were taught by their elders and put through various ordeals in the process of moving from childhood to adulthood. When the essential tasks of this liminal stage were completed, Kunta Kinte returned to the village, but not to his former place. He had become a man, and so he left his former house to establish his own home.

The Liminal Stage

It is the liminal stage that most concerns us here. Those who enter the liminal stage exist outside the normal society, and they relinquish all of the normal social roles. All social distinctions are eliminated; all rights and responsibilities are stripped away. One result of this escape from the social structure is usually an intense experience of unity and comradeship, since it is often social roles and expectations that maintain barriers between people. With a radical equality, there are few distinctions to keep people apart.

This deep experience of community stands in contrast to, and in tension with, the normal social structure. Such experiences give life and vitality to a structure that can become moribund, and the structure gives form to the vitality, channeling and preserving the possibility of such community experiences. But the intense experience of community is also a threat to the structure, for it defies all convention and pattern. If left unchecked, it could easily lead to social chaos. On the other hand, the social structure can prevent such experiences from happening at all if it becomes too rigid and too insistent on maintaining status distinctions and proper roles at all times. The struggle between these two was well illustrated in the sixties with the "hippie rebellion" and our society's often violent response to it. The hippies challenged the social structure by spurning traditional jobs and housing, by defying drug laws, and by blurring male/female distinctions. Many in our society reacted vehemently to the threat. Eventually the hippie communes took on more structure and became more conventional, but the movement also brought some new life into our culture.

Liturgy on the Threshold

It can be very enlightening to view liturgy as a liminal experience. As we noted earlier, when the assembly gathers for worship, all social status distinctions must be left at the door. Here all are equal in the sight of God. The usual social roles do not matter. And the experience of community is central to worship, but it is dependent on whether we really do leave those things that separate us outside. We enter this experience, this space and time that are in the world but not of the world, in order to encounter the Lord who is both immanent and transcendent. There is always a certain ambiguity about the worship experience because it is in this marginal or liminal context. The worshiping community stands on the threshold, with one foot in this world and one foot in the kingdom.

The assembly enters into this threshold experience in order to open itself to the encounter with the Lord. The liturgical celebration is deliberately intended to be out of the ordinary and beyond the usual routine of life. This, of course, stands in contrast to the enculturation of the liturgy, which draws from the daily experiences, and it represents the transcendent side of the polarity. This discontinuity with the daily routine can break open our shells and enable us to experience life, the universe, and God in a new way. This is one of the values of ancient, inherited forms in worship. They can set us free from the constraints our society imposes on us and enable us to envision another way of living.

Kingdom Play

Several writers have described the liturgy as an experience of "playing kingdom." The liturgy enacts an alternative vision of life. During worship we seek to relate to God and to one another according to the values and standards of the kingdom of God. We seek to experience what life would be like if the kingdom were fully present in our world and not just partially realized. We try to experience the fullness of Christian communion, with God and with all our brothers and sisters. Our own daily experience of life makes it pain-fully obvious that the principles of the kingdom are not the principles on which our society operates. Yet we are called to live by kingdom values and to do this in the world, not just in worship.

The experience of worship itself, then, involves an implicit judgment upon our world and the way it operates and structures itself. The liminal experience always critiques the social structure, and an experience of God's kingdom confronts us with a call to conver-sion. The liturgical experience should renew our vision and strengthen our resolve to live out that vision in our daily lives. We are called to build up the kingdom in our world, to move from the ritual experience of the kingdom to the challenging and often frustrating task of transforming the world according to the values of the gospel.

This liminal type of experience is also what we seek in all forms of prayer, and the lessons of the liturgy can be applied to our personal prayer as well. Often our prayer will benefit from having a special place for prayer, which we come to recognize as our own "sacred space" or threshold space. We need to establish some means of creating discontinuity from our routine, of breaking out of the ordinary, so that we are open to the possibility of a real encounter. Sometimes the use of inherited, traditional forms or methods of prayer can be valuable. It is also often helpful to deliberately lay aside our social roles and responsibilities during our time at prayer, to seek an experience that transcends them and revitalizes them.

But a spirituality of this type can be dangerous. To deliberately open oneself to such an encounter places

one in immediate jeopardy of being changed by the experience. If I really discover what the kingdom means, I
may have to change my whole life. If I really come to
understand what is wrong with our usual way of living,
I may have to become a prophet to my friends and
neighbors. I might end up being a protester against injustice in its many contemporary forms. This kind of
spirituality could get me into a lot of trouble!

So, indeed, it could. So it did for Jesus and for
many others before and since. But if it does, then both
we and our world will be the better for it. Worship and
working for justice, playing kingdom and building
kingdom are intimately related. A true liturgical
spirituality will embrace both with the fervor that
comes only from the experience of God's presence and
love. In a sense, the whole of Christian life is lived on
the threshold. We have here no lasting city, no place to
lay our head. We live in an in-between time, for the
kingdom has already come but is not yet here in its
fullness. The liturgical experience of the liminal state
should teach us how to live with this ambiguity at the
same time as it impels us to do all we can to move our
world over the threshold and into that new world and
new age that Jesus promised.

Reflection Questions

1. When was the last time I had a really significant encounter with the Lord? What fostered that meeting?
   What words can I use to describe the experience?

2. Can I remember any experiences when I seemed to be
   "where heaven and earth meet"? What fostered that experience? How did it affect me?

3. What experiences of community stand out in my
   memory? What made them so powerful? How did they
   affect my life?

4. What social roles do I play in my current life-situation?
   How much am I bound by those roles? Can I escape
   from them? How often do I step outside them, outside
   the expectations of the social structure?

5. Have I seen the liturgy as an experience of the kingdom
   of God? Does it help me bring the kingdom closer in my
   daily life?

6. Does my experience of worship impel me to work for a
   better world, for a more just society?

7. Do I have a special place for personal prayer? Would
   such a space help me to pray better? What styles and
   methods of prayer open me most to a true encounter
   with the Lord?

A Pattern for Spontaneity

WITH THE ADVENT of women's liberation, more and more men are finding themselves in the kitchen. One such husband had started dinner one evening before his wife returned from work. On her arrival she pointed out that he should have cut off the ends of the ham before he put it in the oven to bake. When he asked why, she admitted that she didn't know the reason, but that's the way her mother always did it. Intrigued, he called her mother, who in turn said she always did it because *her* mother had done so. Finally they called her grandmother and explained their question. The grandmother laughed and answered, "Oh, I always cut off the ends of the ham because my roasting pan was too small!"

Sometimes we forget why we do things, and this can happen in church as easily as in the kitchen. One of the most frequent critiques of formal worship heard in recent years has been a complaint against ritual. Liturgy has been seen by some as nothing more than a collection of outdated rituals that have little or no meaning in the present age. And even among those who see a value in formal worship, there has been a tendency to reject ritual patterns as inimical to the true spontaneity that should mark our relationship with the Lord.

66

There is no question that the liturgical tradition out of which I write is a tradition of ritual. Our worship follows a generally consistent pattern, with many elements that are unvarying and repetitive. Some other Christian groups have preferred a less structured form of prayer, especially in the "free Church" tradition. But the "liturgical" Churches have seen great value in a consistent pattern of worship. This does not mean a totally rigid and unvarying worship service, for there are numerous opportunities in most liturgies for variety and the inclusion of elements especially suitable for the particular time and situation of a given assembly.

Ritual Pattern

For the most part, however, the liturgical tradition is a tradition of patterned prayer, and it is worth our while to examine this fact to see what value it has for the development of our spirituality. We noted in the last chapter that the liturgy exists to foster the encounter with God, but that encounter can never really be programmed or captured in any ritual pattern. It cannot be ensured, for we do not control the Lord. The function of the ritual pattern is simply to provide a framework within which the encounter can occur. The ritual can help to create the necessary space and time for an encounter. It can help to open us to the possibility of meeting the Lord by inviting us into the realm of the liminal where God may be found. We have the assurance of Christ's presence when we gather in his name because of his promise, but whether that presence will result in a real encounter for the worshipers cannot be controlled.

It is important to note, however, that the very ex-

perience of the repetitive pattern can open us to the encounter. Far from being an obstacle to the spontaneous
experience of the Lord's presence, repetition can be a
vital aid. When the pattern of celebration is always
changing, it is difficult to enter deeply into the experience because one must be continually attentive to
the pattern itself, not knowing quite what to expect
next. A repeated pattern, on the other hand, can
become as comfortable as the proverbial old shoe, a
framework in which we can relax and allow ourselves
to enter into the whole experience on deeper and deeper
levels over time. When I already know the melody of a
hymn, I can really hear the words; when I am very
familiar with the words, I can understand more and
more of the meaning they contain; and when I have
deeply appropriated the meaning, I can focus more
totally on the Lord to whom they point.

Spontaneity

Another way to say this is to say that the experience
of a repeated pattern can free the worshiper for the experience of contemplation. This dynamic is important in
personal prayer as well. Both the Eastern mantra and
the Western rosary are designed to take advantage of
the power of repetition to block out distractions and
foster a contemplative experience. True spontaneity in
prayer is often fostered, paradoxically, by a comfortable, traditional pattern.

This is important not only in an individual experience of prayer but also in the overall perspective of our
spiritual life. We need spontaneity in our relationship
with the Lord, but this will most likely be achieved if
we have a consistent pattern of prayer, spiritual

reading, journal keeping, etc. We all desire those over-powering moments of God's presence, and we long for the spontaneous impulse to pray and praise God. But these moments are gifts from the Lord that are not within our control. We cannot arrange them, earn them, or achieve them by our spiritual exercises. But a consistent schedule of time for prayer and a comfort-able pattern in our approach to prayer can free us to be open for the gift when it comes. A consistent pattern of prayer can help us to enter into that space where God may be met, and it can keep us attentive to God so that we will be able to enter into the encounter when God offers it.

The Danger of Routine

At the same time, it must be admitted that there is a real danger that confronts all who worship and pray in a familiar ritual. It is the danger that we might let the pattern become an end in itself. The routine can be-come a rut, and if we get too comfortable with it, we may get stuck in it. We are all subject to the temptation to prefer security over risk, for we all wish to be in control of our own lives.

We get into trouble when this desire leads us to think that we can control God. We may end up telling God, in effect, how and where the divine encounter must take place if it is to take place at all. Chances are, when we give in to this temptation, the encounter will not take place at all, for our God refuses to be con-trolled. God's Spirit blows where God wills, not where we will. Becoming familiar with God's usual ways of dealing with us, meeting with us, and speaking to us must not close us to God's surprises. For our God is a

God of surprises, and in the divine presence we can never be comfortably secure. To pray is always a risk; to invoke the presence is to invite surprise, for God is truly incomprehensible. "For my thoughts are not your thoughts, nor are your ways my ways, says the Lord" (Isaiah 55:8).

Beyond times of prayer, we are confronted with the same tension. There is need for a pattern in our lives. All virtues are good habits, built up by constant repetition of responses to the gospel. We strive to build up a pattern of holiness, a consistency about how we treat others, a constancy in our loving and caring and serving others in the Lord's name. We continually seek to determine the Lord's will for us and then strive to live according to God's word on a consistent basis. At the same time, we should always remain aware that our God is unpredictable. What God asks of us can, and likely will, change, usually when we least expect it and are least willing to let go of the pattern to which we have become accustomed.

It is both psychologically and spiritually healthy to leave room in our lives and our habits for the unexpected, to stay open to the possibility that our structure of life will be disturbed and rearranged by a new encounter with the Lord. And it is important to remember that the appointment God has set up with us may not be in a church or in our prayer space; it may well be on the road or at work or at home or at school or wherever it is that we don't expect God to show up! God can come anywhere and at any time; it would be tragic to miss such a meeting simply because we had become too attached to the pattern of our dealings with God in the past.

If we achieve such a balance between consistency and spontaneity in our relationship with the Lord, we might well discover that all the other relationships in our lives begin to share that balance. People, too, are unpredictable, because ultimately they are mysterious. We like to think that we can figure others out, categorize them, and know what to expect from them. Some people we see as dependable and helpful; we can count on them. Others are always cheerful; we expect joy from them. Some are close friends; we trust that they will understand us. But if we leave no room for the unexpected in such relationships, we are bound to be disappointed, for no human is as consistent as our image of him or her would suggest.

Conversely, the child who is always a discipline problem, the friend who never returns a call, the repeating criminal and others whom we judge negatively can truly surprise us with their unexpected goodness—but only if we remain open to such a possibility. Even nature often surprises us with unexpected changes in weather, an unnoticed flower that bursts into bloom, or a startled deer that crosses the trail in front of us. A pattern of consistency coupled with an openness to the spontaneous can be a healthy basis for dealing with all aspects of life lived in union with a God who is faithful yet full of surprises.

Reflection Questions

1. Have I recognized the pattern in our worship? Do the parts fit together and make sense to me?

2. Do I experience the "sameness" of the liturgy week after week as boring or consoling? Does it burden me with monotony or free me for prayer?

3. How much pattern have I built into my own prayer life? Do I pray at regular times, in the same place, with the same prayers?

4. How open am I to finding God in unexpected places at unscheduled times?

5. When was the last time I deeply experienced God's presence with me? Was it in a regular time of prayer/worship or in an unexpected situation?

6. How structured is my life? Do I follow a very regular routine? When was the last time I did something really spontaneous?

7. Do I "pigeonhole" people very often? Can I think of some people who have surprised me by their actions or reactions lately?

8. Am I truly open to God's surprises in my life? Do I allow God to deal with me freely or only according to God's "usual" ways?

9. What parts of my life could use more structure, more pattern, more regularity? Where do I need more freedom, more spontaneity?

The Times of Our Lives

MUCH ATTENTION has been given in recent years to the art of storytelling. Numerous workshops have been offered, courses have been taught, books have been written, and a national society has even been organized. And all the time, the authors, speakers, and teachers have been telling us that storytelling is one of the most natural things to do when people gather! Certainly anyone can improve one's skills for such an art, but storytelling doesn't really require special training. It happens whenever people get together and begin to share what has been going on in their lives. It happens whenever old friends reminisce about old times. It happens whenever one generation shares its story with the next. It happens whenever the family gathers to celebrate a birthday or an anniversary. It happens whenever the community observes a civil holiday like Thanksgiving or the Fourth of July. And it happens whenever people gather in church.

Because the form our storytelling takes in church has become rather structured, it's just possible to not notice that it's a story we tell. The Liturgy of the Word, which is part of the Eucharist and most other sacraments and liturgies we celebrate, is really a form

of storytelling. We read the stories of those who have
gone before us, in the belief that they have something
to say to us today and that they are somehow our
stories as well as those of our ancestors. We recall the
great figures of our history: Abraham, Moses, David,
Solomon, Isaiah, Jeremiah, Ezekiel, Ruth, Esther, John
the Baptist, Mary, Peter, Paul, and of course, Jesus, the
most illustrious of our ancestors. We retell, too, the
stories they told—the colorful predictions of the prophets, the radical parables of Jesus, the sermons of Paul.
And in retelling the past, we come to understand the
present and sense our proper course for the future.

Myth

The stories we tell are really in the category of
myth, but *myth* is a word we often misunderstand. We
tend to think of it as just a fairy tale, pure fantasy with
no relation to reality. But myth is an important bearer
of truth in all cultures, both ancient and modern. Myth
is the storyteller's way of communicating ultimate truth.
Some cultures rely on abstract thought to talk about
beauty, goodness, truth, the purpose of life, and other
ultimate concerns; others rely on stories to talk about
the same subjects. But even very philosophical societies
have their myths, usually much older and more popular
than the musings of the philosophers. These myths may
or may not have a direct relationship to what we call
historical fact, but they have a deep and immediate
relationship to the truth, which is deeper than mere
facts. So it is with the stories we tell in church. Some
are more clearly historical than others, but all of them
are true at a level that is deeper and more important
than historical data.

Myth is important to any culture, society, or group because it defines the communal identity. As the myth is retold, we remember who we are. We get in touch with our roots and recall the vision that has guided our group and our kind. The myth is intimately related to the ritual we celebrate, too. On the one hand, the myth specifies the meaning of the rites, since the gestures and actions we perform could mean many things in themselves. On the other hand, the ritual is an enfleshing of the myth; it is the myth in action form and helps to bring the myth to life and make it effective in the present.

In telling the myth and enacting the ritual, the past is brought into the present in an effective way. Both myth and ritual are in the realm of the symbolic, and so they partake of the mystery-laden nature of the symbol. They not only point to and depict the events of the past, but somehow make them present. Christians, like their ancestors the Jews, believe that the liturgical celebration truly brings us into contact with the saving events of our history. This is not to deny their historical character, but it is to insist that they have a dimension that transcends time, since they are ultimately acts of an eternal God. The Jews were taught to celebrate the Passover "as if you yourselves had been led forth from Egypt," because the Lord continues to work his saving deeds in the present (see Deuteronomy 5:2-3). In a similar way, Christians believe that the sacrifice of Jesus by which we are saved is effective in the present because Christ is "forever victim, forever priest," offering an eternal sacrifice that transcends the limits of time.

Our View of the Past

An appreciation of this rich dimension of our worship surely must affect the way we look at the past. Our culture is one that has valued history very little; only in the last few years have trends begun to focus on the preservation of historical neighborhoods and the search for family roots. Our experience of worship reminds us that the past is not only important in itself, but that it has a very real effect on the present. Those who do not remember the past are not only condemned to repeat it, but they are also condemned to a rootless and shallow life. The confusion of the amnesia victim can remind us how important our memories are for knowing who we are. So, too, a society that does not value its memories weakens its sense of identity.

A deeper respect for the value of history would also lead us to a richer appreciation of the gifts of the aged in our midst. It is no secret that our culture has idolized youth and ignored the wisdom of age. The old are a rich source for the present, for they carry within them the tales of the past. Their memories can enrich us and enable us to understand how we came to be where we are today. Our experience of worship ought to teach us how to value the past without becoming stuck there, to treasure our roots precisely because they enable us to grow in the present.

The liturgy also teaches us about the future. Another sense of the remembering that is involved in worship is that God remembers the deeds of the past and therefore continues the divine work of salvation in the present and the future. Thus our remembering is the basis for hope about where the future can go. As Queen Eleanor put it in the movie *Lion in Winter*, "In a world where carpenters get resurrected, anything is possible!" It is because we know God's faithfulness to the promises of the past that we can easily trust God's word for our future. Remembering, therefore, is not an exercise in nostalgia nor an arcane interest in archaeology. It is rather a matter of bringing together the past, the present, and the future in a way that allows the future to be built creatively upon the past.

All Time Is Sacred

The sense of time that the liturgy conveys, then, is a sense of time as sacred. All time—past, present, and future—is embraced in God's eternal present. "All time belongs to him and all the ages" we sing at the Easter Vigil. All time is the arena of God's activity. In the Christian perspective there is not really a distinction between "sacred time" and "profane time." We do observe holy days and feasts, but all days are days lived in God's presence and under God's will.

It is apparent that many people do not yet understand this point, however, since we continue to hear the complaint that the Church should stick to religious matters and keep its nose out of politics. The assumption seems to be that God has nothing to say to us about the course of history in our own time—as if it were really our own time and not God's time. Those who shape our history and the history of future generations desperately need to hear the word of the Lord to them, and the Church has an obligation to proclaim Christ's Lordship over all time and all history.

In our personal lives, too, the liturgy challenges us to see all time as God's time. Our own personal histories contain the record of God's dealings with us.

Telling our own story can be a powerful way to re-member God's favor in the past and to rekindle our hope for that same powerful divine love in the future. It is an important part of Christian spirituality to accept God's dominion over every minute of the day, every day of our lives. All the time we are given is a gift from the Lord, and we are called to use it for God's glory. Since God is the Lord of all time and is present in all time, the divine presence might be revealed to us at any time, not just in times of prayer and worship. Thus, from another dimension of the worship experi-ence, we receive a reminder to be open to the surprises of God in our life.

Liturgical Year

This sense of all time as sacred is also reflected in the Church's celebration of the liturgical year. The year is marked by the annual round of feasts and seasons. Each season is different, both in nature and in the liturgy, yet it is the same Lord who is worshiped and celebrated. A liturgical spirituality will be constantly at-tuned to the seasons of the liturgical cycle. Both our prayers and the general focus of our consciousness should vary from season to season. Advent is a time of waiting and longing, while Christmas invites us to new birth. Lent calls us to reform, repent, and renew our baptismal commitment, while Easter celebrates the newness of life with unrestrained joy. Ordinary time is a time for growth and reflection upon the Lord's teaching, while every major feast day invites us to break forth in praise and festivity.

Our prayer ought to reflect these changing moods and emphases, but so should the rest of our life. Times of celebration ought to be truly festive—all day, not just in church. They are days for dressing up and feasting, for enjoying life to the full. Our work schedules and commitments may restrict us somewhat, but there are always ways to enter into even ordinary events with a spirit of festivity. Maybe it's only singing aloud on the way to work or having wine with dinner, but feasts and seasons of joy are meant to uplift our whole life. And so, too, with all of the liturgical seasons; the tone and mood of our worship should carry over to all the moments of the day so that all time is spent in God's presence.

This cycle of seasons and feasts also reminds us that the liturgy tends to view time differently than our culture. Scholars use the Greek words *chronos* and *kairos* to designate two different types of time. *Chronos* is clock time, second after second, minute after minute, the inexorable march of time. *Kairos,* on the other hand, is the appropriate time, the right time for something, the proper time. It is *kairos*-time that gives meaning and definition to the *chronos.* These are the times we remember, the times by which we mark our histories.

To enter into *kairos*-time and to celebrate the significance of such special moments can be a freeing experience. We are too often dominated by clock time and feel trapped by its tyranny. We live with one eye on the clock, and we frequently hear complaints that there is not enough time. We live under the pressure of deadlines and time clocks, and we can easily feel oppressed by time. To really celebrate is to throw off this tyranny and enter fully into the moment, to know that it is time to rejoice or weep or repent or give thanks, no matter where the hands of the clock point. We cannot, of course, ignore the demands of time, but the liturgy reminds us that some times are more important than others and thus can help us keep a healthier perspective on the time God allots us.

Reflection Questions

1. What stories of the Bible are important to me? Why? What do they tell me about my own story?

2. What is my own story? Could I write an autobiography? Would the Lord's presence be evident in my story?

3. How deeply do I value the past? How much respect do I have for the aged?

4. Do I have good memories of my own past? How do my memories, good or bad, affect my attitude toward my own personal future?

5. How much of my time belongs to the Lord? Do I divide my life into compartments and allow God into only some of them?

6. Does the liturgical year provide a context for my own prayer and spirituality? Do I celebrate feasts and seasons in my life beyond the time I spend at worship?

A Living Sacrifice

THE OLD ARAB was near death, and he called his chief aides to his bedside. "After I die," he said, "I want all the proper Muslim rites carried out. And then I want my body to be buried in Israel." Shocked, his aides protested, "But you have always hated Israel. They are our bitter enemies. You have spent your whole life fighting against them." "All of that is true," he admitted, "but you must remember that they have the best resurrection rate in the world."

The death and resurrection of Jesus stands as the turning point of all human history. The liturgical year finds its center point in this paschal mystery, for every Christian liturgy revolves around this central event of our redemption. This mystery is also the proper focus of a true liturgical spirituality.

It is important to understand this mystery as deeply as we can. One of the first things to realize is that it is an integral reality. The death and resurrection of Jesus are not two separate events that simply happen to follow one another in chronological order; they are like two sides of the same coin, and it is the whole mystery that is redemptive. St. Paul says that "Christ was handed over to death for our sins and raised up for our

81

justification" (Romans 4:25). The two events are one act of salvation and are inseparable. Another way to express this is to say that the death-resurrection of Jesus was his Passover (hence, *paschal* mystery), his passing from this world to the Father (see John 13:1). He passed through death to new life and to total union with the Father.

The Sacrifice of Jesus

Since at least the time of the writing of the Epistle to the Hebrews, this paschal mystery has been seen in terms of sacrifice. Various theories have been put forward through the centuries about the meaning of the term *sacrifice* as it relates to Jesus' Passover, and even more ink has been spilled over the question of how his sacrifice is related to the liturgy. What I wish to present here is an understanding of these matters that I find spiritually fruitful; I leave it to the theologians of the different traditions to continue their search for a consensus on the issues.

It seems critical at the outset to remember that the Epistle to the Hebrews is very clear on the fact that there is only one sacrifice in the New Testament, the sacrifice of Jesus (Hebrews 10:1-18). No other sacrifice is necessary, nor is any other sacrifice acceptable for our salvation. Yet the Church has long seen the Eucharist as sacrifice, and the Scriptures speak of offering our lives as a spiritual sacrifice. If these traditions are to be harmonized, then, these "other" sacrifices must really be a sharing in the one sacrifice of Jesus.

Sharing His Sacrifice

It is possible for us to share in the sacrifice of Christ because that sacrifice has an eternal dimension. It is important at this point to sort out the central core of that sacrifice, for that is what we are invited to share. The goal of any sacrifice, religious anthropologists tell us, is to achieve union with the divinity. For Jesus this was expressed as union with his Father, that full union in glory that was the result of his Passover. The central theme of his sacrifice, therefore, might best be seen in the agony in the garden of Gethsemane. Jesus' prayer in the garden expresses the core of his sacrifice: ". . . not my will but yours be done" (Luke 22:42). That total union of his will with the Father's will is central—and eternal. The sacrifice took shape in history on Calvary and at the tomb, but that historical expression of it is not eternal. Christ died once for all; he will never die again (see Romans 6:9-10). But his submission to the Father's will is eternal; he remains in union with the Father, forever victim, forever priest.

It is this submission we are called to share in the liturgy. In every Eucharist we tell the story and enact the rite. Christ is present in his eternal act of union with the Father, and we are invited to join him in that submission. The Church is the body of Christ and is continually challenged to "have that mind in you which was in Christ Jesus" (Philippians 2:5). This is what it means to share in the Eucharist. This is what it means to say "Amen" to the Eucharistic Prayer, which proclaims the death and resurrection of the Lord. This is what it means to be baptized—to take on the pattern of Jesus' life, death and resurrection as our own pattern. This is truly a call to share in the sacrifice of Christ.

To celebrate liturgy, especially baptism and the Eucharist, is to commit ourselves to a style of life based on the paschal mystery. It is the hallmark of our lives, recurring over and over again in numerous variations like the recurrent theme of a symphony. Again and again God calls us to die to self and live for others, to put to death the old life of sin and live the new life of holiness, to embrace the cross that we might be raised to resurrection life. The very number of times and the multiplicity of ways that the liturgy expresses this theme should give us a hint that the theme is to be central to our whole lives. Though there is only one sacrifice, our participation in it takes many forms, and to share in it fully takes us a lifetime.

Conversion

This participation, this growth into the pattern of Jesus, is what is meant by "conversion." To convert our lives, or more accurately, to allow God to convert us, is an ongoing process, not the work of a moment. There may well be those powerful moments when the Lord touches our lives and impels us to change quickly, but even those moments are part of a larger process and need to be confirmed and strengthened by an ongoing growth.

Conversion is a constant dynamic, and one that is central to the liturgy. We do not go to church because we are fully converted. We do not go to church if we are not converted at all. We go to church because we are *being* converted by God's power day by day. Week after week we celebrate the Eucharist, giving thanks for the conversion that has taken place and committing ourselves to continue on the road of conversion. Each week we strive to enter more fully into the paschal mystery, to die a bit more to sin and live a bit more like Christ. That's why we need to go every week!

If conversion were a "one-shot deal," we would need the Church only until that event had occurred. But conversion is a long-term, daily process, and the liturgy calls us to embrace the journey fully day by day. This is, in one sense, the most fundamental participation in the sacrifice of Jesus. Paul expresses it well in Romans 12:1-2: "I beg you through the mercy of God to offer your bodies as a living sacrifice holy and acceptable to God, your spiritual worship. Do not conform yourselves to this age but be transformed by the renewal of your mind, so that you may judge what is God's will, what is good, pleasing and perfect."

All Christian spirituality, then, has this as its purpose: to allow God to continue the work of converting us into Christ's image. This demands of us that we continually strive to drop all those false identities with which we hide and protect our true self. Conversion is not a matter of rejecting our own identity in order to take on the identity of Jesus; it is rather a matter of discovering our true identity and finding out that we are already made in Christ's image. All that we have to surrender, all that must be put to death in us is false: false goals that will not satisfy us, false security that will not save us, false loves that will not bring us unity, false values that will not reward us, false hopes that will fail us, and above all, a false identity that does not allow us to become who we really are, who God made us to be.

Natives in the Pacific reportedly capture monkeys with an ingenious trap. They drain coconuts, making a hole large enough for the monkey to put an open hand into it, but too small for a closed fist. Then they put a few pebbles into the coconuts. The monkeys shake the coconuts and, hearing the pebbles, thrust in a hand to grasp them. Unable to withdraw from the trap without letting go of the pebbles, the monkeys are easily caught.

How silly it seems for a monkey to lose its freedom because of clinging to worthless pebbles. Yet we often are just as foolish, clinging to false treasures even though they prevent us from truly becoming free and becoming ourselves. Conversion is not a negative dynamic of self-rejection but a positive and hope-filled process of coming open. It comes about to the extent that we have come to know and believe in God's love for us, and it results in a growing ability to love others in God's name. Growth in love may be painful, and, in fact, it usually is. But the pain is a joyful pain, for like the pain of labor, it signals a new birth and new life. Spirituality is simply the process of loving God and other people and all creation; it is simply the way we allow God to convert us. This is the goal of all prayer as well as all liturgy: to dwell in the love of God long enough and deeply enough to learn to love as God loves.

What is true in spirituality is true of all life. New life does come out of death, growth does result from pain lovingly embraced. By its focus on the paschal mystery, the liturgy constantly reminds us of the necessary connection between the cross and the resurrection. This should help us to reject the temptation, so common in our culture, to avoid pain at all costs. We cannot afford to delude ourselves into thinking that growth should be easy, love should be painless, and happiness should be constant. The cross stands as constant witness that life involves suffering, but the resurrection stands as witness that new life can come from even the deepest pain. By embracing this mystery we come more and more to live a life of real love, a life that is in itself a continual sacrifice of praise to the Lord.

Reflection Questions

1. Is the death and resurrection of Jesus the real center point of my own faith?

2. When I think of the sacrifice of Jesus, do I think mostly of his death or his resurrection or both?

3. What does Christ's sacrifice mean to me? How does it affect my life?

4. When we gather for Eucharist, do I experience it as a sharing in the sacrifice of Christ? How can I get more in tune with that reality?

5. Can I think of any times recently when God called me to die to self and live more for others? Did that dying bring new life for me and/or for others?

6. Where am I on my conversion journey? What is God calling me to change at this point in my life?

7. What false identities do I use to hide my real self? What will it take for me to let go of these false images?

8. How willing am I to embrace the cross? How much do I trust God to bring me to new life through the cross?

Sharing the Shared Life of God

WHEN I WAS A CHILD in parochial school, the parish priest used to come to our religion class from time to time and quiz us on what we had learned. One day he asked the class if we knew what prayer Christians customarily used at the end of other prayers. He was a bit disappointed by our ignorance, I suspect, because at that point in our lives, none of us knew of the tradition of ending the psalms and other prayers with the doxology, the prayer of praise to the Trinity. It is a simple prayer but it expresses profound praise: "Glory be to the Father, and to the Son, and to the Holy Spirit, as it was in the beginning, is now and ever shall be, world without end. Amen."

This is a good way to conclude our prayer and also a good focus to conclude our consideration of the different dimensions of the liturgical experience. We have considered a variety of aspects of worship thus far, many of which we share not only with other Christian denominations, but also with people of the Jewish faith. But Christian worship is also distinctively non-Jewish, for all Christian worship is Trinitarian in its form and its focus.

Trinitarian Liturgy

In its form the liturgy customarily addresses prayer *to* the Father, *through* the Son, and *in* the Spirit. This is not a mere matter of style or variety in language; it reflects the community's recognition of the different ways we relate to the three Persons of the Trinity. This stands in contrast to the doxology quoted above, in which the three Persons are addressed identically. Compare that with the wording of the doxology at the end of the Eucharistic Prayer: "*Through* him, *with* him, *in* him, *in* the unity of the Holy Spirit, all glory and honor is *yours,* almighty Father, for ever and ever." The liturgy maintains Jesus' own custom of praying to the Father, who is the source of all that is. Prayers are addressed through the Son, for Christians recognize Christ as the true mediator between heaven and earth. Jesus stands forever before the throne of grace, making intercession for us (see Romans 8:34), and it is only in union with his prayer that our prayers become acceptable to God.

The custom of prayer *in* the Spirit witnesses to two different but related traditions in the early liturgy. Sometimes the prayer was offered "through Christ in the Holy Spirit" and at other times "through Christ in the holy Church." This does not, of course, suggest an identity between the Spirit and the Church, but it does remind us of the deep awareness in the early Church that it was the Spirit who formed the Church and bound it together in love. Where the Church was, the Spirit was, for without the presence of the unifying Spirit, there would be no Church. The Church was the assembly of those who lived (and prayed) in the power of the Spirit of God. So, to pray in the Church was always to pray in the Spirit, or as other prayers put it, "in the unity of the Holy Spirit."

This Trinitarian character of our worship also witnesses to the Trinitarian nature of creation and redemption. The Trinity is the source and focus of worship because the Trinity is the source and goal of all Christian life. In the beginning there was only God. All else that is flows from the Godhead and is in some sense an extension of the life of the Trinity. And the goal of life is to be caught up fully in the life shared by the Father, the Son, and the Spirit.

The theologians of the East were especially fond of language that speaks of the "divinizing" power of grace. An oft-repeated insight says that the divinity became human so that humans might become divine. One might quibble with the precision of the language here, but we are probing into mystery, and the language of the poet may be most appropriate in such a realm. In any case, it is clear that we are invited to share the life of the Trinity. This is the meaning of grace. This is the significance of the divine indwelling. This is the eternal life that Christ offers us.

The Trinity in Prayer and in Life

All of our prayer, then, ought to take place in the context of the Trinity. I do not mean that we must always follow the liturgy's pattern of language and worry about the proper use of prepositions. Even the liturgy itself finds room for a few prayers addressed to Christ and to the Spirit, and personal prayer has always enjoyed a greater variety than the formal ritual prayer of the community. What is important for a liturgical spirituality is that our prayer should be mindful of the presence of the Trinity in our lives.

This should mean some variety in the focus of our prayer, for we do relate to God in different ways, according to the different Persons of the Trinity. We tend to view the Father as the source, the creator, the one to whom thanks and praise are always due, the one who holds us in existence. The Son, especially the incarnate Son, is addressed as redeemer and savior, as one like us who shared our troubles, as brother and friend. The Spirit is experienced especially as the God within, the one closer to us than we are to ourselves, the one who inspires and instructs and guides. The incredible richness of the Godhead should lead to a rich variety in our prayer, even though it is still the one God whom we address.

This consciousness of the Trinity should also pervade our daily lives. We are called to carry on the work of God in our world. This includes a share in the work of creation, as we give new form and shape to the universe by our effort and labor and creativity. Our work on the farm and in the factory, at the stove and in the mechanic's shop, at the piano and in the artist's studio are all ways in which we share in the creative work of the Father. We are also commissioned to carry on the redemptive work of Christ. Our efforts to spread the Good News by word and example, to reach out to those in need, to struggle against injustice in its myriad forms, and to embrace suffering for the sake of others are all ways in which the work of redemption continues. The work of the Spirit is especially the sanctification of the world. We share in that work whenever we truly encounter another in love and let God's love touch the other through us, whenever we pray for others, whenever we teach another to pray or share prayer with them, whenever we reveal the power of God at work in us and thus invite others into the divine presence.

To share the life of the Trinity also reminds us that we are made for community. Though the analogy cannot be drawn exactly, the doctrine of the Trinity presents God as a community in the Godhead. Since we are made in God's image, we come to our fulfillment only in relationships with others. We are truly made for love, and we become ourselves only insofar as we open ourselves to love and to be loved. One whose spirituality is Trinitarian will not only be willing to enter into communion with others, but will also seek to foster the development of true community among all people.

All of this we are called to do if our spirituality is to be truly Christian and truly liturgical, for such a spirituality must be a share in the life and work of the Trinity. To share that life is the whole purpose of spirituality, and to share in the divine life is to share in the divine work. It is a great and exalted vocation to which we have been called. May our response to that call be rich and full, so that full glory and praise may be given to the Father through the Son in the Spirit, both now and forever.

Reflection Questions

1. How Trinitarian is my worship? Am I aware of the liturgy's approach to Father, Son, and Spirit?

2. How Trinitarian is my personal prayer? Do I have a personal relationship with each of the three divine Persons?

3. Which Person of the Trinity seems farthest from me? Could I benefit from focusing my prayer more often on that Person?

4. How am I carrying on the creative work of God the Father? In what ways could I share in the work of creation more fully?

5. How am I carrying on the redemptive work of Christ? In what ways could I deepen my sharing in his work?

6. How do I share in the sanctifying work of the Spirit? Can I do more to work for the sanctification of the world today?

7. How can I foster the growth of community in our world, in my own household, and with my friends, as well as among all people and races and nations?

The Liturgy of Life

THROUGHOUT THIS SERIES of meditations on the various aspects of the liturgical experience, we have been assuming an integral connection between liturgy and daily life. If such an integration were the common experience of contemporary Christians, this little book might be largely superfluous. Much of the work yet to be accomplished in the process of liturgical and spiritual renewal revolves around the restoration of this basic connection.

Celebration of Life

Liturgy is meant to be the celebration of life as a whole. It is a celebration of God's activity in the world, a joyful act of praise and thanksgiving for the wonderful works of God in the past and in our own time. Like any human celebration, liturgy offers us a break in the everyday routine of life, a chance to step back and view life from a different perspective. If liturgy is different from daily existence, it is not because it is totally separate from the rest of life, but because it is a more intense experience of that life and of its meaning. Celebrations can bring life into focus and renew our understanding of what we are about. At the same time, celebration always involves an affirmation of that life and issues in new strength to face the challenges of life.

Too often people place the blame for the separation of liturgy from life on the side of the liturgy. Certainly it is true that much of our formal worship in the past, and still too often in the present, left too little room for integrating daily concerns and contemporary styles of expression. But it seems equally true that we have failed far too often to make the required effort to bring the experience of liturgy to bear on the issues and concerns we face throughout the rest of the week. When the sign of peace was reintroduced into the Eucharist, for example, I heard numerous complaints that it was hypocritical, since we were being asked to share this symbol in church with people we would ignore the rest of the week. My response at first was to agree that this was a problem, but after a while I began to realize that what needed to be changed was not the liturgy but the way we treated one another after church, beginning in the parking lot!

The Richness of the Liturgy

That realization might well have been the seed that was planted years ago and has been growing slowly within me until it led to these reflections. Week by week, year by year, I have become more and more aware of the tremendous richness of the liturgy and the great potential it harbors for enriching the lives of all who share in it. As this awareness has grown, I have also become saddened by the realization that so many people participate in the liturgy week after week and seem to be largely untouched by the experience. People comment if the homily was good that Sunday, or if the music was well done, or if the presider was warm and prayerful. All of these are obviously important, but I am deeply convinced that the very form and structure of the experience of liturgy has much to teach us in itself.

Perhaps many more people are being formed by the liturgy than one can tell by observation. The Spirit of God works in quiet and hidden ways. But I have also come to believe that much of the richness of the liturgy can be unlocked only through prayerful reflection on what we are about when we gather for worship. It is in order to foster this process that I have undertaken the task of putting these reflections on paper. It is my hope that this little book will not be put on the shelf once it is read, but that it will be re-read slowly, one chapter at a time, as a basis for extended reflection in a context of prayer. Thus it might serve as a key to unlock more of the richness that the experience of the liturgy can provide.

A Life of Celebration

Many of us have grown up with a work ethic that exhorts us to keep our nose close to the grindstone. One insightful, if amateur, poet has challenged the wisdom of that ethic:

> If your nose is close to the grindstone rough
> And you hold it down there long enough,
> In time you'll say there's no such thing
> As brooks that babble and birds that sing.
> These three will all your world compose:
> Just you, the stone, and your darned old nose!*

---

*Copyright 1958 Christian Century Foundation. Reprinted by permission from the February 12, 1958 issue of *The Christian Century*.

A deepening understanding of the connections between life and liturgy should lead not only to liturgical
celebrations that are more lively but also to a life that
is more of a celebration. We have said that our lives
are to be our sacrifice of praise. They are also to be
celebration, for they are lived in the warmth of God's
love and filled with signs of God's presence. Our first
response to God's initiative is praise and thanksgiving,
which make a good foundation for celebrating life. The
word of God addressed to us calls us together as a
community, to search for truth together and to be re-
sponsible for one another. The invitation to be part of
this community of love is cause for celebration.

As we learn to recognize the face of God enfleshed
in all the people and things around us, we will often be
impelled to rejoice in God's loving care. So, too, those
moments when we suddenly encounter the infinite God
in the midst of the pattern of our lives inspire us to
burst forth in joyful song. Whenever we remember
God's wonders in the past and in our own lives, we are
filled with hope, especially as we realize that God is
really changing us deeply through the grace of conversion and making us whole. And to recognize that God
has invited us to share the very life of the Trinity
should lead us to live in constant wonder and awe.

The Hasidic Jews say that if a person fulfills all the
commandments, he or she is admitted to heaven. But if
that person has felt no delight on earth, he or she will
feel none in heaven either. Finally such a person begins
to grumble, "And they make such a big deal about
paradise!" With that, such a one is thrown out! One of
the best ways to prepare for paradise is to learn to
celebrate life here on earth to the full.

I once received a greeting card with a picture of a young person skipping along the crest of a ridge with the sun low in the sky beyond the ridge. Across the card were these words: "To the wise, life is a festival." May God lead us all to such wisdom.

Reflection Questions

1. Do I experience the liturgy as a celebration and affirmation of life? Is it more of a celebration of life at some times than at others? What makes the difference?

2. How can I bring the liturgy to bear on my daily life more fully? What would need to change in my life to be in tune with the liturgy?

3. Would it be helpful to my own spirituality to reflect prayerfully on the texts of the liturgy before and/or after the time of worship?

4. Have my reading and reflection on this book been helpful in mining the riches of the liturgy? How has my relationship with the Lord grown? How has my spirituality been affected by these reflections?

5. How much do I experience life itself as a celebration? What can I do to make it more awe-filled and wonderful?

Rev. Lawrence E. Mick, currently pastor of St.
Patrick's Church, Glynnwood, Ohio, and consultant to
the Office for Worship of the Cincinnati Archdiocese,
received degrees in philosophy and theology from the
Athenaeum of Ohio, and a master's degree in liturgical
studies from the University of Notre Dame (1972). He is
an associate member of the North American Academy of
Liturgy and a member of the Liturgical Conference and
the North American Forum on the Catechumenate. He
has written numerous articles on liturgical topics for
Pastoral Life, Today's Parish, the *New Catholic
Encyclopedia,* the *Chicago Catechumenate,* and *Christian
Initiation Resources.* Father Mick has also served as a
campus minister at Wright State University, Dayton,
Ohio, and as a member of a retreat team at Maria Stein
Retreat Center, Maria Stein, Ohio.